This book is dedicated to Yves Klein, Annachiara, and Andrea.— FG

Phaidon Press Inc.
65 Bleecker Street
New York, NY 10012

Phaidon Press Limited
Regent's Wharf
All Saints Street
London N1 9PA

phaidon.com

This edition © 2019 Phaidon Press Limited
First published as *Yves Klein* by Fausto Gilberti
© Fausto Gilberti, © Maurizio Corraini s.r.l.
Published by arrangement with Maurizio Corraini s.r.l.

Text set in Raisonne Demibold and Fugue Regular

ISBN 978 183866 014 7
001-0719

Printed in China

Picture credit: © Succession Yves Klein c/o ADAGP,
Paris and DACS, London 2019

YVES
KLEIN

Painted Everything Blue and Wasn't Sorry.

Fausto Gilberti

It was raining in Paris and Yves was thinking.

He was thinking about the stunning blue sky
he saw while lying on the beach. He imagined
that the sky was one of his paintings.
His most beautiful one!

Yves was an artist.

Yves decided that, from then on, he would paint everything in blue! But not any old blue – Yves wanted a unique blue, his own blue. He mixed powder, glue, and some other secret ingredients. He mixed and tested and mixed and tested until he found the blue that he was looking for. It was a bright, vivid blue, and it reminded him of the sky and sea. He called it "International Klein Blue"!

Yves was so happy that he immediately created eleven all-blue paintings that looked exactly alike. He put them in a case and set off for Italy. He wanted to display them at an exhibition in Milan.

Yves hung them on the gallery walls and put a different price on each one. Even though all the paintings were almost identical, Italian collectors looked at all of them carefully, trying to find the smallest differences.

Yves Klein's blue phase had begun.

Yves covered canvases,
sponges, globes, branches,
and art gallery floors
with his International
Klein Blue paint.

He loved blue so much that he even made a blue drink for guests to sip as they looked at his art.

He imagined that it made their pee blue, too!

One time, as a celebration of blue, Yves released
a thousand and one blue balloons into the Parisian sky!

Yves liked to be busy. He never stopped for a minute.

When he wasn't working on his art, Yves trained and taught judo. He was very good, and became a black belt.

He also liked creating games. Sometimes he spent his evenings racing cockroaches with his friends!

Yves was inventive: he was always thinking about new ways of making art.

"What if I painted with … fire?" And that's when Yves came up with fire paintings.

"What if I painted with ... water?"
And that's when Yves decided to let the rain
fall onto a canvas covered with blue powder.

"What if I painted with … wind?"
And that's when Yves tied a freshly
painted blue canvas to the roof of
his car and drove at full speed from
Paris to Nice!

Yves also had people use their bodies to paint. They would cover themselves in fresh blue paint, International Klein Blue, and imprint their bodies on his canvases.

He even painted using smoke by setting off huge firecrackers!

Yves continued to surprise his audience in other artistic ways: he wrote an entire symphony using just one note, followed by twenty minutes of silence...

He created a photograph that made it look like he could fly (it was really a trick photograph) . . .

He designed a rocket to fly over Paris
and into space, never to return . . .

He even dared to be different at his own wedding, where he wore a knight's uniform, and a sword!

Yves Klein was a unique and innovative artist. He was one of the first artists ever to use fire, wind, empty space, and silence in his work.

People around the world remember him not only for his blue paintings, but also for the daring ways he chose to create.

Bravo, Yves!

MORE ABOUT YVES KLEIN

Yves Klein was one of France's most inventive artists. He was born in Nice, in the south of France, in 1928. He never went to art school, but he learned a lot about art from his parents, who were both artists.

While he was young, Yves went around the world to Italy, England, Ireland, Spain, and Japan. In Japan, he learned judo and became an expert, earning a black belt.

When he returned from Japan, Yves started making art. Instead of drawing pictures of the people and things around him, he focused on creative ideas. He made art in new and sometimes shocking ways. For example, he most famously loved blue so much that he created a special blue himself and named it International Klein Blue (or IKB for short), and painted many of his works in only blue. He also experimented with other unusual ways of creating, using fire, smoke, water, wind, sound, photography, and even empty space.

Yves fell in love with a German artist called Rotraut Uecker and married her in 1962, but sadly he died of a heart attack in Paris later that year. He was only 34 years old. Although he died at a young age, he left behind many artworks that continue to inspire artists around the world to experiment and invent new ways of creating art.

This painting by Yves Klein is called *Untitled Blue Monochrome, (IKB 79)*. IKB stands for International Klein Blue! It was painted with dry pigment and synthetic resin on gauze and mounted on panel. The painting is 47(w) x 55(h) inches / 140(h) x 120(w) centimeters large, and can be seen in person at the Tate Modern museum in London.